MW01205365

## Thank you for being our valued customer

We will be grateful if you shared this happy experience in the online review section.
This helpes us to continue providing great products
and helps potential buyers to make a confident decision.

### check my booklets collection on amazon under this name
**AUTHOR NAME:** *DogVaccination Publishing Record*

**Brand Name: Zebra Lines Publishing**

© 2021 COPYRIGHT PROTECTED BY ZEBRA LINES ™

The Moral Rights Of The Author Have Been Asserted.all Rights Reserved.
No Part Of This Book May Be Reproduced In Any Form On By An Electronic
Or Mechanical Means, Including Information Storage And Retrieval
Systems, Without Permission In Writing From The Publisher, Except By A
Reviewer Who May Quote Brief Passages In A Review.

# PHOTO OF ME AND MY PET

# THIS BOOK BELONGS TO

**NAME :** ..................................................................................

**ADDRESS :** ..............................................................................

**PHONE :** ................................................................................

# PET DETAILS

**NAME :**

**BREED :**

**BIRTHDAY :**

**GENDER :**

**ID CHIP :**

**BREED REGISTRATION :**

**ALLERGIES :**

**SKIN COLOR:**

**EYE COLOR:**

**WEIGHT:**

**MEDICAL CONDITIONS:**

**SPECIAL MARKINGS:**

**FAVORITE TOYS:**

## NOTES :

# PET OWNER

**NAME :**

**SURNAME :**

**ADDRESS :**

**POSTCODE :**

**CITY :**

**PHONE NUMBER :**

**EMAIL :**

## NOTES :

## VET. INFO

**NAME :**

**PHONE :**

**EMAIL :**

**ADDRESS :**

## HOSPITAL INFO

**NAME/BUSINESS :**

**PHONE :**

**EMAIL :**

**ADDRESS :**

## PET INSURANCE DETAILS

**INSURANCE COMPANY:**

**POLICY TYPE:**

**POLICY NUMBER:**

**CONTACT:**

**DETAILS:**

# MY PET IMMUNIZATION RECORDS

| DATE | AGE | TYPE | GIVEN BY | NEXT DUE |
|------|-----|------|----------|----------|
|      |     |      |          |          |
|      |     |      |          |          |
|      |     |      |          |          |
|      |     |      |          |          |
|      |     |      |          |          |
|      |     |      |          |          |
|      |     |      |          |          |
|      |     |      |          |          |
|      |     |      |          |          |
|      |     |      |          |          |
|      |     |      |          |          |

# MY PET
# WELLNESS
# HISTORY

| DATE | AGE | TYPE | PHYSICAL OBSERVATION | MEDICATION |
|------|-----|------|---------------------|------------|
|      |     |      |                     |            |
|      |     |      |                     |            |
|      |     |      |                     |            |
|      |     |      |                     |            |
|      |     |      |                     |            |
|      |     |      |                     |            |
|      |     |      |                     |            |
|      |     |      |                     |            |
|      |     |      |                     |            |
|      |     |      |                     |            |
|      |     |      |                     |            |

# MY PET
# DAILY CARE
# CHECKLIST

| DATE | FOOD | WATER | WALK | BATH |
|------|------|-------|------|------|
|      |      |       |      |      |
|      |      |       |      |      |
|      |      |       |      |      |
|      |      |       |      |      |
|      |      |       |      |      |
|      |      |       |      |      |
|      |      |       |      |      |
|      |      |       |      |      |
|      |      |       |      |      |
|      |      |       |      |      |
|      |      |       |      |      |

# MY PET
# IMMUNIZATION
# RECORDS

| DATE | AGE | TYPE | GIVEN BY | NEXT DUE |
|------|-----|------|----------|----------|
|      |     |      |          |          |
|      |     |      |          |          |
|      |     |      |          |          |
|      |     |      |          |          |
|      |     |      |          |          |
|      |     |      |          |          |
|      |     |      |          |          |
|      |     |      |          |          |
|      |     |      |          |          |
|      |     |      |          |          |
|      |     |      |          |          |

# MY PET
# WELLNESS
# HISTORY

| DATE | AGE | TYPE | PHYSICAL OBSERVATION | MEDICATION |
|------|-----|------|----------------------|------------|
|      |     |      |                      |            |
|      |     |      |                      |            |
|      |     |      |                      |            |
|      |     |      |                      |            |
|      |     |      |                      |            |
|      |     |      |                      |            |
|      |     |      |                      |            |
|      |     |      |                      |            |
|      |     |      |                      |            |
|      |     |      |                      |            |
|      |     |      |                      |            |

# MY PET
# DAILY CARE
# CHECKLIST

| DATE | FOOD | WATER | WALK | BATH |
|------|------|-------|------|------|
|      |      |       |      |      |
|      |      |       |      |      |
|      |      |       |      |      |
|      |      |       |      |      |
|      |      |       |      |      |
|      |      |       |      |      |
|      |      |       |      |      |
|      |      |       |      |      |
|      |      |       |      |      |
|      |      |       |      |      |
|      |      |       |      |      |

# MY PET
# IMMUNIZATION
# RECORDS

| DATE | AGE | TYPE | GIVEN BY | NEXT DUE |
|------|-----|------|----------|----------|
|      |     |      |          |          |
|      |     |      |          |          |
|      |     |      |          |          |
|      |     |      |          |          |
|      |     |      |          |          |
|      |     |      |          |          |
|      |     |      |          |          |
|      |     |      |          |          |
|      |     |      |          |          |
|      |     |      |          |          |
|      |     |      |          |          |

# MY PET WELLNESS HISTORY

| DATE | AGE | TYPE | PHYSICAL OBSERVATION | MEDICATION |
|------|-----|------|----------------------|------------|
|      |     |      |                      |            |
|      |     |      |                      |            |
|      |     |      |                      |            |
|      |     |      |                      |            |
|      |     |      |                      |            |
|      |     |      |                      |            |
|      |     |      |                      |            |
|      |     |      |                      |            |
|      |     |      |                      |            |
|      |     |      |                      |            |
|      |     |      |                      |            |

# MY PET
# DAILY CARE
# CHECKLIST

| DATE | FOOD | WATER | WALK | BATH |
|------|------|-------|------|------|
|      |      |       |      |      |
|      |      |       |      |      |
|      |      |       |      |      |
|      |      |       |      |      |
|      |      |       |      |      |
|      |      |       |      |      |
|      |      |       |      |      |
|      |      |       |      |      |
|      |      |       |      |      |
|      |      |       |      |      |
|      |      |       |      |      |

# MY PET IMMUNIZATION RECORDS

| DATE | AGE | TYPE | GIVEN BY | NEXT DUE |
|---|---|---|---|---|
| | | | | |
| | | | | |
| | | | | |
| | | | | |
| | | | | |
| | | | | |
| | | | | |
| | | | | |
| | | | | |
| | | | | |
| | | | | |

# MY PET WELLNESS HISTORY

| DATE | AGE | TYPE | PHYSICAL OBSERVATION | MEDICATION |
|------|-----|------|----------------------|------------|
|      |     |      |                      |            |
|      |     |      |                      |            |
|      |     |      |                      |            |
|      |     |      |                      |            |
|      |     |      |                      |            |
|      |     |      |                      |            |
|      |     |      |                      |            |
|      |     |      |                      |            |
|      |     |      |                      |            |
|      |     |      |                      |            |
|      |     |      |                      |            |

# MY PET
# DAILY CARE
# CHECKLIST

| DATE | FOOD | WATER | WALK | BATH |
|------|------|-------|------|------|
|      |      |       |      |      |
|      |      |       |      |      |
|      |      |       |      |      |
|      |      |       |      |      |
|      |      |       |      |      |
|      |      |       |      |      |
|      |      |       |      |      |
|      |      |       |      |      |
|      |      |       |      |      |
|      |      |       |      |      |
|      |      |       |      |      |

# MY PET IMMUNIZATION RECORDS

| DATE | AGE | TYPE | GIVEN BY | NEXT DUE |
|------|-----|------|----------|----------|
|      |     |      |          |          |
|      |     |      |          |          |
|      |     |      |          |          |
|      |     |      |          |          |
|      |     |      |          |          |
|      |     |      |          |          |
|      |     |      |          |          |
|      |     |      |          |          |
|      |     |      |          |          |
|      |     |      |          |          |
|      |     |      |          |          |

# MY PET WELLNESS HISTORY

| DATE | AGE | TYPE | PHYSICAL OBSERVATION | MEDICATION |
|------|-----|------|----------------------|------------|
|      |     |      |                      |            |
|      |     |      |                      |            |
|      |     |      |                      |            |
|      |     |      |                      |            |
|      |     |      |                      |            |
|      |     |      |                      |            |
|      |     |      |                      |            |
|      |     |      |                      |            |
|      |     |      |                      |            |
|      |     |      |                      |            |
|      |     |      |                      |            |

# MY PET
# DAILY CARE
# CHECKLIST

| DATE | FOOD | WATER | WALK | BATH |
|------|------|-------|------|------|
|      |      |       |      |      |
|      |      |       |      |      |
|      |      |       |      |      |
|      |      |       |      |      |
|      |      |       |      |      |
|      |      |       |      |      |
|      |      |       |      |      |
|      |      |       |      |      |
|      |      |       |      |      |
|      |      |       |      |      |
|      |      |       |      |      |

# MY PET
# IMMUNIZATION
# RECORDS

| DATE | AGE | TYPE | GIVEN BY | NEXT DUE |
|------|-----|------|----------|----------|
|      |     |      |          |          |
|      |     |      |          |          |
|      |     |      |          |          |
|      |     |      |          |          |
|      |     |      |          |          |
|      |     |      |          |          |
|      |     |      |          |          |
|      |     |      |          |          |
|      |     |      |          |          |
|      |     |      |          |          |
|      |     |      |          |          |

# MY PET
# WELLNESS
# HISTORY

| DATE | AGE | TYPE | PHYSICAL OBSERVATION | MEDICATION |
|------|-----|------|----------------------|------------|
|      |     |      |                      |            |
|      |     |      |                      |            |
|      |     |      |                      |            |
|      |     |      |                      |            |
|      |     |      |                      |            |
|      |     |      |                      |            |
|      |     |      |                      |            |
|      |     |      |                      |            |
|      |     |      |                      |            |
|      |     |      |                      |            |
|      |     |      |                      |            |

# MY PET
# DAILY CARE
# CHECKLIST

| DATE | FOOD | WATER | WALK | BATH |
|------|------|-------|------|------|
|      |      |       |      |      |
|      |      |       |      |      |
|      |      |       |      |      |
|      |      |       |      |      |
|      |      |       |      |      |
|      |      |       |      |      |
|      |      |       |      |      |
|      |      |       |      |      |
|      |      |       |      |      |
|      |      |       |      |      |
|      |      |       |      |      |

# MY PET
# IMMUNIZATION
# RECORDS

| DATE | AGE | TYPE | GIVEN BY | NEXT DUE |
|------|-----|------|----------|----------|
|      |     |      |          |          |
|      |     |      |          |          |
|      |     |      |          |          |
|      |     |      |          |          |
|      |     |      |          |          |
|      |     |      |          |          |
|      |     |      |          |          |
|      |     |      |          |          |
|      |     |      |          |          |
|      |     |      |          |          |
|      |     |      |          |          |

# MY PET WELLNESS HISTORY

| DATE | AGE | TYPE | PHYSICAL OBSERVATION | MEDICATION |
|------|-----|------|----------------------|------------|
|      |     |      |                      |            |
|      |     |      |                      |            |
|      |     |      |                      |            |
|      |     |      |                      |            |
|      |     |      |                      |            |
|      |     |      |                      |            |
|      |     |      |                      |            |
|      |     |      |                      |            |
|      |     |      |                      |            |
|      |     |      |                      |            |
|      |     |      |                      |            |

# MY PET
# DAILY CARE
# CHECKLIST

| DATE | FOOD | WATER | WALK | BATH |
|------|------|-------|------|------|
|      |      |       |      |      |
|      |      |       |      |      |
|      |      |       |      |      |
|      |      |       |      |      |
|      |      |       |      |      |
|      |      |       |      |      |
|      |      |       |      |      |
|      |      |       |      |      |
|      |      |       |      |      |
|      |      |       |      |      |
|      |      |       |      |      |

# MY PET
# IMMUNIZATION
# RECORDS

| DATE | AGE | TYPE | GIVEN BY | NEXT DUE |
|------|-----|------|----------|----------|
|      |     |      |          |          |
|      |     |      |          |          |
|      |     |      |          |          |
|      |     |      |          |          |
|      |     |      |          |          |
|      |     |      |          |          |
|      |     |      |          |          |
|      |     |      |          |          |
|      |     |      |          |          |
|      |     |      |          |          |
|      |     |      |          |          |

# MY PET WELLNESS HISTORY

| DATE | AGE | TYPE | PHYSICAL OBSERVATION | MEDICATION |
|------|-----|------|----------------------|------------|
|      |     |      |                      |            |
|      |     |      |                      |            |
|      |     |      |                      |            |
|      |     |      |                      |            |
|      |     |      |                      |            |
|      |     |      |                      |            |
|      |     |      |                      |            |
|      |     |      |                      |            |
|      |     |      |                      |            |
|      |     |      |                      |            |
|      |     |      |                      |            |

# MY PET
# DAILY CARE
# CHECKLIST

| DATE | FOOD | WATER | WALK | BATH |
|------|------|-------|------|------|
|      |      |       |      |      |
|      |      |       |      |      |
|      |      |       |      |      |
|      |      |       |      |      |
|      |      |       |      |      |
|      |      |       |      |      |
|      |      |       |      |      |
|      |      |       |      |      |
|      |      |       |      |      |
|      |      |       |      |      |
|      |      |       |      |      |

# MY PET
# IMMUNIZATION
# RECORDS

| DATE | AGE | TYPE | GIVEN BY | NEXT DUE |
|------|-----|------|----------|----------|
|      |     |      |          |          |
|      |     |      |          |          |
|      |     |      |          |          |
|      |     |      |          |          |
|      |     |      |          |          |
|      |     |      |          |          |
|      |     |      |          |          |
|      |     |      |          |          |
|      |     |      |          |          |
|      |     |      |          |          |
|      |     |      |          |          |

# MY PET WELLNESS HISTORY

| DATE | AGE | TYPE | PHYSICAL OBSERVATION | MEDICATION |
|------|-----|------|----------------------|------------|
|      |     |      |                      |            |
|      |     |      |                      |            |
|      |     |      |                      |            |
|      |     |      |                      |            |
|      |     |      |                      |            |
|      |     |      |                      |            |
|      |     |      |                      |            |
|      |     |      |                      |            |
|      |     |      |                      |            |
|      |     |      |                      |            |
|      |     |      |                      |            |

# MY PET
# DAILY CARE
# CHECKLIST

| DATE | FOOD | WATER | WALK | BATH |
|------|------|-------|------|------|
|      |      |       |      |      |
|      |      |       |      |      |
|      |      |       |      |      |
|      |      |       |      |      |
|      |      |       |      |      |
|      |      |       |      |      |
|      |      |       |      |      |
|      |      |       |      |      |
|      |      |       |      |      |
|      |      |       |      |      |
|      |      |       |      |      |

# MY PET
# IMMUNIZATION
# RECORDS

| DATE | AGE | TYPE | GIVEN BY | NEXT DUE |
|------|-----|------|----------|----------|
|      |     |      |          |          |
|      |     |      |          |          |
|      |     |      |          |          |
|      |     |      |          |          |
|      |     |      |          |          |
|      |     |      |          |          |
|      |     |      |          |          |
|      |     |      |          |          |
|      |     |      |          |          |
|      |     |      |          |          |
|      |     |      |          |          |

# VET. VISIT NOTES

# VET. VISIT NOTES

# VET. VISIT NOTES

# VET. VISIT NOTES

# VET. VISIT NOTES

# VET. VISIT NOTES

# MY PET IMMUNIZATION RECORDS

| DATE | AGE | TYPE | GIVEN BY | NEXT DUE |
|------|-----|------|----------|----------|
|      |     |      |          |          |
|      |     |      |          |          |
|      |     |      |          |          |
|      |     |      |          |          |
|      |     |      |          |          |
|      |     |      |          |          |
|      |     |      |          |          |
|      |     |      |          |          |
|      |     |      |          |          |
|      |     |      |          |          |
|      |     |      |          |          |

# MY PET
# WELLNESS
# HISTORY

| DATE | AGE | TYPE | PHYSICAL OBSERVATION | MEDICATION |
|------|-----|------|----------------------|------------|
|      |     |      |                      |            |
|      |     |      |                      |            |
|      |     |      |                      |            |
|      |     |      |                      |            |
|      |     |      |                      |            |
|      |     |      |                      |            |
|      |     |      |                      |            |
|      |     |      |                      |            |
|      |     |      |                      |            |
|      |     |      |                      |            |
|      |     |      |                      |            |

# MY PET
# DAILY CARE
# CHECKLIST

| DATE | FOOD | WATER | WALK | BATH |
|------|------|-------|------|------|
|      |      |       |      |      |
|      |      |       |      |      |
|      |      |       |      |      |
|      |      |       |      |      |
|      |      |       |      |      |
|      |      |       |      |      |
|      |      |       |      |      |
|      |      |       |      |      |
|      |      |       |      |      |
|      |      |       |      |      |
|      |      |       |      |      |

# MY PET IMMUNIZATION RECORDS

| DATE | AGE | TYPE | GIVEN BY | NEXT DUE |
|------|-----|------|----------|----------|
|      |     |      |          |          |
|      |     |      |          |          |
|      |     |      |          |          |
|      |     |      |          |          |
|      |     |      |          |          |
|      |     |      |          |          |
|      |     |      |          |          |
|      |     |      |          |          |
|      |     |      |          |          |
|      |     |      |          |          |
|      |     |      |          |          |

# MY PET WELLNESS HISTORY

| DATE | AGE | TYPE | PHYSICAL OBSERVATION | MEDICATION |
|------|-----|------|----------------------|------------|
|      |     |      |                      |            |
|      |     |      |                      |            |
|      |     |      |                      |            |
|      |     |      |                      |            |
|      |     |      |                      |            |
|      |     |      |                      |            |
|      |     |      |                      |            |
|      |     |      |                      |            |
|      |     |      |                      |            |
|      |     |      |                      |            |
|      |     |      |                      |            |

# MY PET
# DAILY CARE
# CHECKLIST

| DATE | FOOD | WATER | WALK | BATH |
|------|------|-------|------|------|
|      |      |       |      |      |
|      |      |       |      |      |
|      |      |       |      |      |
|      |      |       |      |      |
|      |      |       |      |      |
|      |      |       |      |      |
|      |      |       |      |      |
|      |      |       |      |      |
|      |      |       |      |      |
|      |      |       |      |      |
|      |      |       |      |      |

# MY PET
# IMMUNIZATION
# RECORDS

| DATE | AGE | TYPE | GIVEN BY | NEXT DUE |
|------|-----|------|----------|----------|
|      |     |      |          |          |
|      |     |      |          |          |
|      |     |      |          |          |
|      |     |      |          |          |
|      |     |      |          |          |
|      |     |      |          |          |
|      |     |      |          |          |
|      |     |      |          |          |
|      |     |      |          |          |
|      |     |      |          |          |
|      |     |      |          |          |

# MY PET
# WELLNESS
# HISTORY

| DATE | AGE | TYPE | PHYSICAL OBSERVATION | MEDICATION |
|------|-----|------|----------------------|------------|
|      |     |      |                      |            |
|      |     |      |                      |            |
|      |     |      |                      |            |
|      |     |      |                      |            |
|      |     |      |                      |            |
|      |     |      |                      |            |
|      |     |      |                      |            |
|      |     |      |                      |            |
|      |     |      |                      |            |
|      |     |      |                      |            |
|      |     |      |                      |            |

# MY PET
# DAILY CARE
# CHECKLIST

| DATE | FOOD | WATER | WALK | BATH |
|------|------|-------|------|------|
|      |      |       |      |      |
|      |      |       |      |      |
|      |      |       |      |      |
|      |      |       |      |      |
|      |      |       |      |      |
|      |      |       |      |      |
|      |      |       |      |      |
|      |      |       |      |      |
|      |      |       |      |      |
|      |      |       |      |      |
|      |      |       |      |      |

# MY PET
# IMMUNIZATION
# RECORDS

| DATE | AGE | TYPE | GIVEN BY | NEXT DUE |
|------|-----|------|----------|----------|
|      |     |      |          |          |
|      |     |      |          |          |
|      |     |      |          |          |
|      |     |      |          |          |
|      |     |      |          |          |
|      |     |      |          |          |
|      |     |      |          |          |
|      |     |      |          |          |
|      |     |      |          |          |
|      |     |      |          |          |
|      |     |      |          |          |

# MY PET WELLNESS HISTORY

| DATE | AGE | TYPE | PHYSICAL OBSERVATION | MEDICATION |
|------|-----|------|----------------------|------------|
|      |     |      |                      |            |
|      |     |      |                      |            |
|      |     |      |                      |            |
|      |     |      |                      |            |
|      |     |      |                      |            |
|      |     |      |                      |            |
|      |     |      |                      |            |
|      |     |      |                      |            |
|      |     |      |                      |            |
|      |     |      |                      |            |
|      |     |      |                      |            |

# MY PET
# DAILY CARE
# CHECKLIST

| DATE | FOOD | WATER | WALK | BATH |
|------|------|-------|------|------|
|      |      |       |      |      |
|      |      |       |      |      |
|      |      |       |      |      |
|      |      |       |      |      |
|      |      |       |      |      |
|      |      |       |      |      |
|      |      |       |      |      |
|      |      |       |      |      |
|      |      |       |      |      |
|      |      |       |      |      |
|      |      |       |      |      |

# MY PET IMMUNIZATION RECORDS

| DATE | AGE | TYPE | GIVEN BY | NEXT DUE |
|------|-----|------|----------|----------|
|      |     |      |          |          |
|      |     |      |          |          |
|      |     |      |          |          |
|      |     |      |          |          |
|      |     |      |          |          |
|      |     |      |          |          |
|      |     |      |          |          |
|      |     |      |          |          |
|      |     |      |          |          |
|      |     |      |          |          |
|      |     |      |          |          |

# MY PET WELLNESS HISTORY

| DATE | AGE | TYPE | PHYSICAL OBSERVATION | MEDICATION |
|------|-----|------|----------------------|------------|
|      |     |      |                      |            |
|      |     |      |                      |            |
|      |     |      |                      |            |
|      |     |      |                      |            |
|      |     |      |                      |            |
|      |     |      |                      |            |
|      |     |      |                      |            |
|      |     |      |                      |            |
|      |     |      |                      |            |
|      |     |      |                      |            |
|      |     |      |                      |            |

# MY PET
# DAILY CARE
# CHECKLIST

| DATE | FOOD | WATER | WALK | BATH |
|------|------|-------|------|------|
|      |      |       |      |      |
|      |      |       |      |      |
|      |      |       |      |      |
|      |      |       |      |      |
|      |      |       |      |      |
|      |      |       |      |      |
|      |      |       |      |      |
|      |      |       |      |      |
|      |      |       |      |      |
|      |      |       |      |      |
|      |      |       |      |      |

# MY PET
# WELLNESS
# HISTORY

| DATE | AGE | TYPE | PHYSICAL OBSERVATION | MEDICATION |
|------|-----|------|---------------------|------------|
|      |     |      |                     |            |
|      |     |      |                     |            |
|      |     |      |                     |            |
|      |     |      |                     |            |
|      |     |      |                     |            |
|      |     |      |                     |            |
|      |     |      |                     |            |
|      |     |      |                     |            |
|      |     |      |                     |            |
|      |     |      |                     |            |
|      |     |      |                     |            |

# MY PET
# DAILY CARE
# CHECKLIST

| DATE | FOOD | WATER | WALK | BATH |
|------|------|-------|------|------|
|      |      |       |      |      |
|      |      |       |      |      |
|      |      |       |      |      |
|      |      |       |      |      |
|      |      |       |      |      |
|      |      |       |      |      |
|      |      |       |      |      |
|      |      |       |      |      |
|      |      |       |      |      |
|      |      |       |      |      |
|      |      |       |      |      |

# MY PET IMMUNIZATION RECORDS

| DATE | AGE | TYPE | GIVEN BY | NEXT DUE |
|------|-----|------|----------|----------|
|      |     |      |          |          |
|      |     |      |          |          |
|      |     |      |          |          |
|      |     |      |          |          |
|      |     |      |          |          |
|      |     |      |          |          |
|      |     |      |          |          |
|      |     |      |          |          |
|      |     |      |          |          |
|      |     |      |          |          |
|      |     |      |          |          |

# MY PET
# WELLNESS
# HISTORY

| DATE | AGE | TYPE | PHYSICAL OBSERVATION | MEDICATION |
|------|-----|------|----------------------|------------|
|      |     |      |                      |            |
|      |     |      |                      |            |
|      |     |      |                      |            |
|      |     |      |                      |            |
|      |     |      |                      |            |
|      |     |      |                      |            |
|      |     |      |                      |            |
|      |     |      |                      |            |
|      |     |      |                      |            |
|      |     |      |                      |            |
|      |     |      |                      |            |

# MY PET
# DAILY CARE
# CHECKLIST

| DATE | FOOD | WATER | WALK | BATH |
|------|------|-------|------|------|
|      |      |       |      |      |
|      |      |       |      |      |
|      |      |       |      |      |
|      |      |       |      |      |
|      |      |       |      |      |
|      |      |       |      |      |
|      |      |       |      |      |
|      |      |       |      |      |
|      |      |       |      |      |
|      |      |       |      |      |
|      |      |       |      |      |

# MY PET
# IMMUNIZATION
# RECORDS

| DATE | AGE | TYPE | GIVEN BY | NEXT DUE |
|------|-----|------|----------|----------|
|      |     |      |          |          |
|      |     |      |          |          |
|      |     |      |          |          |
|      |     |      |          |          |
|      |     |      |          |          |
|      |     |      |          |          |
|      |     |      |          |          |
|      |     |      |          |          |
|      |     |      |          |          |
|      |     |      |          |          |
|      |     |      |          |          |

# MY PET WELLNESS HISTORY

| DATE | AGE | TYPE | PHYSICAL OBSERVATION | MEDICATION |
|------|-----|------|----------------------|------------|
|      |     |      |                      |            |
|      |     |      |                      |            |
|      |     |      |                      |            |
|      |     |      |                      |            |
|      |     |      |                      |            |
|      |     |      |                      |            |
|      |     |      |                      |            |
|      |     |      |                      |            |
|      |     |      |                      |            |
|      |     |      |                      |            |
|      |     |      |                      |            |

# MY PET
# DAILY CARE
# CHECKLIST

| DATE | FOOD | WATER | WALK | BATH |
|------|------|-------|------|------|
|      |      |       |      |      |
|      |      |       |      |      |
|      |      |       |      |      |
|      |      |       |      |      |
|      |      |       |      |      |
|      |      |       |      |      |
|      |      |       |      |      |
|      |      |       |      |      |
|      |      |       |      |      |
|      |      |       |      |      |
|      |      |       |      |      |

# MY PET IMMUNIZATION RECORDS

| DATE | AGE | TYPE | GIVEN BY | NEXT DUE |
|------|-----|------|----------|----------|
|      |     |      |          |          |
|      |     |      |          |          |
|      |     |      |          |          |
|      |     |      |          |          |
|      |     |      |          |          |
|      |     |      |          |          |
|      |     |      |          |          |
|      |     |      |          |          |
|      |     |      |          |          |
|      |     |      |          |          |
|      |     |      |          |          |

# MY PET WELLNESS HISTORY

| DATE | AGE | TYPE | PHYSICAL OBSERVATION | MEDICATION |
|------|-----|------|----------------------|------------|
|      |     |      |                      |            |
|      |     |      |                      |            |
|      |     |      |                      |            |
|      |     |      |                      |            |
|      |     |      |                      |            |
|      |     |      |                      |            |
|      |     |      |                      |            |
|      |     |      |                      |            |
|      |     |      |                      |            |
|      |     |      |                      |            |
|      |     |      |                      |            |

# MY PET
# DAILY CARE
# CHECKLIST

| DATE | FOOD | WATER | WALK | BATH |
|------|------|-------|------|------|
|      |      |       |      |      |
|      |      |       |      |      |
|      |      |       |      |      |
|      |      |       |      |      |
|      |      |       |      |      |
|      |      |       |      |      |
|      |      |       |      |      |
|      |      |       |      |      |
|      |      |       |      |      |
|      |      |       |      |      |
|      |      |       |      |      |

# MY PET
# IMMUNIZATION
# RECORDS

| DATE | AGE | TYPE | GIVEN BY | NEXT DUE |
|------|-----|------|----------|----------|
|      |     |      |          |          |
|      |     |      |          |          |
|      |     |      |          |          |
|      |     |      |          |          |
|      |     |      |          |          |
|      |     |      |          |          |
|      |     |      |          |          |
|      |     |      |          |          |
|      |     |      |          |          |
|      |     |      |          |          |
|      |     |      |          |          |

# MY PET
# WELLNESS
# HISTORY

| DATE | AGE | TYPE | PHYSICAL OBSERVATION | MEDICATION |
|------|-----|------|----------------------|------------|
|      |     |      |                      |            |
|      |     |      |                      |            |
|      |     |      |                      |            |
|      |     |      |                      |            |
|      |     |      |                      |            |
|      |     |      |                      |            |
|      |     |      |                      |            |
|      |     |      |                      |            |
|      |     |      |                      |            |
|      |     |      |                      |            |
|      |     |      |                      |            |

# MY PET
# DAILY CARE
# CHECKLIST

| DATE | FOOD | WATER | WALK | BATH |
|------|------|-------|------|------|
|      |      |       |      |      |
|      |      |       |      |      |
|      |      |       |      |      |
|      |      |       |      |      |
|      |      |       |      |      |
|      |      |       |      |      |
|      |      |       |      |      |
|      |      |       |      |      |
|      |      |       |      |      |
|      |      |       |      |      |
|      |      |       |      |      |

# MY PET
# IMMUNIZATION
# RECORDS

| DATE | AGE | TYPE | GIVEN BY | NEXT DUE |
|------|-----|------|----------|----------|
|      |     |      |          |          |
|      |     |      |          |          |
|      |     |      |          |          |
|      |     |      |          |          |
|      |     |      |          |          |
|      |     |      |          |          |
|      |     |      |          |          |
|      |     |      |          |          |
|      |     |      |          |          |
|      |     |      |          |          |
|      |     |      |          |          |

# VET. VISIT NOTES

# VET. VISIT NOTES

# VET. VISIT NOTES

# VET. VISIT NOTES

# VET. VISIT NOTES

# VET. VISIT NOTES

# MY PET IMMUNIZATION RECORDS

| DATE | AGE | TYPE | GIVEN BY | NEXT DUE |
|------|-----|------|----------|----------|
|      |     |      |          |          |
|      |     |      |          |          |
|      |     |      |          |          |
|      |     |      |          |          |
|      |     |      |          |          |
|      |     |      |          |          |
|      |     |      |          |          |
|      |     |      |          |          |
|      |     |      |          |          |
|      |     |      |          |          |
|      |     |      |          |          |

# MY PET WELLNESS HISTORY

| DATE | AGE | TYPE | PHYSICAL OBSERVATION | MEDICATION |
|------|-----|------|----------------------|------------|
|      |     |      |                      |            |
|      |     |      |                      |            |
|      |     |      |                      |            |
|      |     |      |                      |            |
|      |     |      |                      |            |
|      |     |      |                      |            |
|      |     |      |                      |            |
|      |     |      |                      |            |
|      |     |      |                      |            |
|      |     |      |                      |            |
|      |     |      |                      |            |

# MY PET
# DAILY CARE
# CHECKLIST

| DATE | FOOD | WATER | WALK | BATH |
|------|------|-------|------|------|
|      |      |       |      |      |
|      |      |       |      |      |
|      |      |       |      |      |
|      |      |       |      |      |
|      |      |       |      |      |
|      |      |       |      |      |
|      |      |       |      |      |
|      |      |       |      |      |
|      |      |       |      |      |
|      |      |       |      |      |
|      |      |       |      |      |

# MY PET
# IMMUNIZATION
# RECORDS

| DATE | AGE | TYPE | GIVEN BY | NEXT DUE |
|------|-----|------|----------|----------|
|      |     |      |          |          |
|      |     |      |          |          |
|      |     |      |          |          |
|      |     |      |          |          |
|      |     |      |          |          |
|      |     |      |          |          |
|      |     |      |          |          |
|      |     |      |          |          |
|      |     |      |          |          |
|      |     |      |          |          |
|      |     |      |          |          |

# MY PET
# WELLNESS
# HISTORY

| DATE | AGE | TYPE | PHYSICAL OBSERVATION | MEDICATION |
|------|-----|------|----------------------|------------|
|      |     |      |                      |            |
|      |     |      |                      |            |
|      |     |      |                      |            |
|      |     |      |                      |            |
|      |     |      |                      |            |
|      |     |      |                      |            |
|      |     |      |                      |            |
|      |     |      |                      |            |
|      |     |      |                      |            |
|      |     |      |                      |            |
|      |     |      |                      |            |

# MY PET
# DAILY CARE
# CHECKLIST

| DATE | FOOD | WATER | WALK | BATH |
|------|------|-------|------|------|
|      |      |       |      |      |
|      |      |       |      |      |
|      |      |       |      |      |
|      |      |       |      |      |
|      |      |       |      |      |
|      |      |       |      |      |
|      |      |       |      |      |
|      |      |       |      |      |
|      |      |       |      |      |
|      |      |       |      |      |
|      |      |       |      |      |

# MY PET
# IMMUNIZATION
# RECORDS

| DATE | AGE | TYPE | GIVEN BY | NEXT DUE |
|------|-----|------|----------|----------|
|      |     |      |          |          |
|      |     |      |          |          |
|      |     |      |          |          |
|      |     |      |          |          |
|      |     |      |          |          |
|      |     |      |          |          |
|      |     |      |          |          |
|      |     |      |          |          |
|      |     |      |          |          |
|      |     |      |          |          |
|      |     |      |          |          |

# MY PET WELLNESS HISTORY

| DATE | AGE | TYPE | PHYSICAL OBSERVATION | MEDICATION |
|------|-----|------|---------------------|------------|
|      |     |      |                     |            |
|      |     |      |                     |            |
|      |     |      |                     |            |
|      |     |      |                     |            |
|      |     |      |                     |            |
|      |     |      |                     |            |
|      |     |      |                     |            |
|      |     |      |                     |            |
|      |     |      |                     |            |
|      |     |      |                     |            |
|      |     |      |                     |            |

# MY PET DAILY CARE CHECKLIST

| DATE | FOOD | WATER | WALK | BATH |
|------|------|-------|------|------|
|      |      |       |      |      |
|      |      |       |      |      |
|      |      |       |      |      |
|      |      |       |      |      |
|      |      |       |      |      |
|      |      |       |      |      |
|      |      |       |      |      |
|      |      |       |      |      |
|      |      |       |      |      |
|      |      |       |      |      |
|      |      |       |      |      |

# MY PET IMMUNIZATION RECORDS

| DATE | AGE | TYPE | GIVEN BY | NEXT DUE |
|------|-----|------|----------|----------|
|      |     |      |          |          |
|      |     |      |          |          |
|      |     |      |          |          |
|      |     |      |          |          |
|      |     |      |          |          |
|      |     |      |          |          |
|      |     |      |          |          |
|      |     |      |          |          |
|      |     |      |          |          |
|      |     |      |          |          |
|      |     |      |          |          |

# MY PET WELLNESS HISTORY

| DATE | AGE | TYPE | PHYSICAL OBSERVATION | MEDICATION |
|------|-----|------|----------------------|------------|
|      |     |      |                      |            |
|      |     |      |                      |            |
|      |     |      |                      |            |
|      |     |      |                      |            |
|      |     |      |                      |            |
|      |     |      |                      |            |
|      |     |      |                      |            |
|      |     |      |                      |            |
|      |     |      |                      |            |
|      |     |      |                      |            |
|      |     |      |                      |            |

# MY PET
# DAILY CARE
# CHECKLIST

| DATE | FOOD | WATER | WALK | BATH |
|------|------|-------|------|------|
|      |      |       |      |      |
|      |      |       |      |      |
|      |      |       |      |      |
|      |      |       |      |      |
|      |      |       |      |      |
|      |      |       |      |      |
|      |      |       |      |      |
|      |      |       |      |      |
|      |      |       |      |      |
|      |      |       |      |      |
|      |      |       |      |      |

# MY PET IMMUNIZATION RECORDS

| DATE | AGE | TYPE | GIVEN BY | NEXT DUE |
|------|-----|------|----------|----------|
|      |     |      |          |          |
|      |     |      |          |          |
|      |     |      |          |          |
|      |     |      |          |          |
|      |     |      |          |          |
|      |     |      |          |          |
|      |     |      |          |          |
|      |     |      |          |          |
|      |     |      |          |          |
|      |     |      |          |          |
|      |     |      |          |          |

# MY PET WELLNESS HISTORY

| DATE | AGE | TYPE | PHYSICAL OBSERVATION | MEDICATION |
|------|-----|------|---------------------|------------|
|      |     |      |                     |            |
|      |     |      |                     |            |
|      |     |      |                     |            |
|      |     |      |                     |            |
|      |     |      |                     |            |
|      |     |      |                     |            |
|      |     |      |                     |            |
|      |     |      |                     |            |
|      |     |      |                     |            |
|      |     |      |                     |            |
|      |     |      |                     |            |

# MY PET
# DAILY CARE
# CHECKLIST

| DATE | FOOD | WATER | WALK | BATH |
|------|------|-------|------|------|
|      |      |       |      |      |
|      |      |       |      |      |
|      |      |       |      |      |
|      |      |       |      |      |
|      |      |       |      |      |
|      |      |       |      |      |
|      |      |       |      |      |
|      |      |       |      |      |
|      |      |       |      |      |
|      |      |       |      |      |
|      |      |       |      |      |

# MY PET WELLNESS HISTORY

| DATE | AGE | TYPE | PHYSICAL OBSERVATION | MEDICATION |
|------|-----|------|----------------------|------------|
|      |     |      |                      |            |
|      |     |      |                      |            |
|      |     |      |                      |            |
|      |     |      |                      |            |
|      |     |      |                      |            |
|      |     |      |                      |            |
|      |     |      |                      |            |
|      |     |      |                      |            |
|      |     |      |                      |            |
|      |     |      |                      |            |
|      |     |      |                      |            |

# MY PET
# DAILY CARE
# CHECKLIST

| DATE | FOOD | WATER | WALK | BATH |
|------|------|-------|------|------|
|      |      |       |      |      |
|      |      |       |      |      |
|      |      |       |      |      |
|      |      |       |      |      |
|      |      |       |      |      |
|      |      |       |      |      |
|      |      |       |      |      |
|      |      |       |      |      |
|      |      |       |      |      |
|      |      |       |      |      |
|      |      |       |      |      |

# MY PET IMMUNIZATION RECORDS

| DATE | AGE | TYPE | GIVEN BY | NEXT DUE |
|------|-----|------|----------|----------|
|      |     |      |          |          |
|      |     |      |          |          |
|      |     |      |          |          |
|      |     |      |          |          |
|      |     |      |          |          |
|      |     |      |          |          |
|      |     |      |          |          |
|      |     |      |          |          |
|      |     |      |          |          |
|      |     |      |          |          |
|      |     |      |          |          |

# MY PET
# WELLNESS
# HISTORY

| DATE | AGE | TYPE | PHYSICAL OBSERVATION | MEDICATION |
|------|-----|------|---------------------|------------|
|      |     |      |                     |            |
|      |     |      |                     |            |
|      |     |      |                     |            |
|      |     |      |                     |            |
|      |     |      |                     |            |
|      |     |      |                     |            |
|      |     |      |                     |            |
|      |     |      |                     |            |
|      |     |      |                     |            |
|      |     |      |                     |            |
|      |     |      |                     |            |

# MY PET
# DAILY CARE
# CHECKLIST

| DATE | FOOD | WATER | WALK | BATH |
|------|------|-------|------|------|
|      |      |       |      |      |
|      |      |       |      |      |
|      |      |       |      |      |
|      |      |       |      |      |
|      |      |       |      |      |
|      |      |       |      |      |
|      |      |       |      |      |
|      |      |       |      |      |
|      |      |       |      |      |
|      |      |       |      |      |
|      |      |       |      |      |

# MY PET
# IMMUNIZATION
# RECORDS

| DATE | AGE | TYPE | GIVEN BY | NEXT DUE |
|------|-----|------|----------|----------|
|      |     |      |          |          |
|      |     |      |          |          |
|      |     |      |          |          |
|      |     |      |          |          |
|      |     |      |          |          |
|      |     |      |          |          |
|      |     |      |          |          |
|      |     |      |          |          |
|      |     |      |          |          |
|      |     |      |          |          |
|      |     |      |          |          |

# MY PET
# WELLNESS
# HISTORY

| DATE | AGE | TYPE | PHYSICAL OBSERVATION | MEDICATION |
|------|-----|------|----------------------|------------|
|      |     |      |                      |            |
|      |     |      |                      |            |
|      |     |      |                      |            |
|      |     |      |                      |            |
|      |     |      |                      |            |
|      |     |      |                      |            |
|      |     |      |                      |            |
|      |     |      |                      |            |
|      |     |      |                      |            |
|      |     |      |                      |            |
|      |     |      |                      |            |

# MY PET
# DAILY CARE
# CHECKLIST

| DATE | FOOD | WATER | WALK | BATH |
|------|------|-------|------|------|
|      |      |       |      |      |
|      |      |       |      |      |
|      |      |       |      |      |
|      |      |       |      |      |
|      |      |       |      |      |
|      |      |       |      |      |
|      |      |       |      |      |
|      |      |       |      |      |
|      |      |       |      |      |
|      |      |       |      |      |

# MY PET
# IMMUNIZATION
# RECORDS

| DATE | AGE | TYPE | GIVEN BY | NEXT DUE |
|------|-----|------|----------|----------|
|      |     |      |          |          |
|      |     |      |          |          |
|      |     |      |          |          |
|      |     |      |          |          |
|      |     |      |          |          |
|      |     |      |          |          |
|      |     |      |          |          |
|      |     |      |          |          |
|      |     |      |          |          |
|      |     |      |          |          |
|      |     |      |          |          |

# MY PET
# WELLNESS
# HISTORY

| DATE | AGE | TYPE | PHYSICAL OBSERVATION | MEDICATION |
|------|-----|------|----------------------|------------|
|      |     |      |                      |            |
|      |     |      |                      |            |
|      |     |      |                      |            |
|      |     |      |                      |            |
|      |     |      |                      |            |
|      |     |      |                      |            |
|      |     |      |                      |            |
|      |     |      |                      |            |
|      |     |      |                      |            |
|      |     |      |                      |            |
|      |     |      |                      |            |

# MY PET DAILY CARE CHECKLIST

| DATE | FOOD | WATER | WALK | BATH |
|------|------|-------|------|------|
|      |      |       |      |      |
|      |      |       |      |      |
|      |      |       |      |      |
|      |      |       |      |      |
|      |      |       |      |      |
|      |      |       |      |      |
|      |      |       |      |      |
|      |      |       |      |      |
|      |      |       |      |      |
|      |      |       |      |      |

# MY PET IMMUNIZATION RECORDS

| DATE | AGE | TYPE | GIVEN BY | NEXT DUE |
|------|-----|------|----------|----------|
|      |     |      |          |          |
|      |     |      |          |          |
|      |     |      |          |          |
|      |     |      |          |          |
|      |     |      |          |          |
|      |     |      |          |          |
|      |     |      |          |          |
|      |     |      |          |          |
|      |     |      |          |          |
|      |     |      |          |          |
|      |     |      |          |          |

# MY PET WELLNESS HISTORY

| DATE | AGE | TYPE | PHYSICAL OBSERVATION | MEDICATION |
|------|-----|------|----------------------|------------|
|      |     |      |                      |            |
|      |     |      |                      |            |
|      |     |      |                      |            |
|      |     |      |                      |            |
|      |     |      |                      |            |
|      |     |      |                      |            |
|      |     |      |                      |            |
|      |     |      |                      |            |
|      |     |      |                      |            |
|      |     |      |                      |            |

# MY PET
# DAILY CARE
# CHECKLIST

| DATE | FOOD | WATER | WALK | BATH |
|------|------|-------|------|------|
|      |      |       |      |      |
|      |      |       |      |      |
|      |      |       |      |      |
|      |      |       |      |      |
|      |      |       |      |      |
|      |      |       |      |      |
|      |      |       |      |      |
|      |      |       |      |      |
|      |      |       |      |      |
|      |      |       |      |      |
|      |      |       |      |      |

# MY PET
# IMMUNIZATION
# RECORDS

| DATE | AGE | TYPE | GIVEN BY | NEXT DUE |
|------|-----|------|----------|----------|
|      |     |      |          |          |
|      |     |      |          |          |
|      |     |      |          |          |
|      |     |      |          |          |
|      |     |      |          |          |
|      |     |      |          |          |
|      |     |      |          |          |
|      |     |      |          |          |
|      |     |      |          |          |
|      |     |      |          |          |
|      |     |      |          |          |

# VET. VISIT NOTES

# VET. VISIT NOTES

# VET. VISIT NOTES

# VET. VISIT NOTES

# VET. VISIT NOTES

# VET. VISIT NOTES

# MY PET
# IMMUNIZATION
# RECORDS

| DATE | AGE | TYPE | GIVEN BY | NEXT DUE |
|------|-----|------|----------|----------|
|      |     |      |          |          |
|      |     |      |          |          |
|      |     |      |          |          |
|      |     |      |          |          |
|      |     |      |          |          |
|      |     |      |          |          |
|      |     |      |          |          |
|      |     |      |          |          |
|      |     |      |          |          |
|      |     |      |          |          |
|      |     |      |          |          |

# MY PET WELLNESS HISTORY

| DATE | AGE | TYPE | PHYSICAL OBSERVATION | MEDICATION |
|------|-----|------|----------------------|------------|
|      |     |      |                      |            |
|      |     |      |                      |            |
|      |     |      |                      |            |
|      |     |      |                      |            |
|      |     |      |                      |            |
|      |     |      |                      |            |
|      |     |      |                      |            |
|      |     |      |                      |            |
|      |     |      |                      |            |
|      |     |      |                      |            |
|      |     |      |                      |            |

# MY PET
# DAILY CARE
# CHECKLIST

| DATE | FOOD | WATER | WALK | BATH |
|------|------|-------|------|------|
|      |      |       |      |      |
|      |      |       |      |      |
|      |      |       |      |      |
|      |      |       |      |      |
|      |      |       |      |      |
|      |      |       |      |      |
|      |      |       |      |      |
|      |      |       |      |      |
|      |      |       |      |      |
|      |      |       |      |      |
|      |      |       |      |      |

# MY PET IMMUNIZATION RECORDS

| DATE | AGE | TYPE | GIVEN BY | NEXT DUE |
|------|-----|------|----------|----------|
|      |     |      |          |          |
|      |     |      |          |          |
|      |     |      |          |          |
|      |     |      |          |          |
|      |     |      |          |          |
|      |     |      |          |          |
|      |     |      |          |          |
|      |     |      |          |          |
|      |     |      |          |          |
|      |     |      |          |          |
|      |     |      |          |          |

# MY PET WELLNESS HISTORY

| DATE | AGE | TYPE | PHYSICAL OBSERVATION | MEDICATION |
|------|-----|------|----------------------|------------|
|      |     |      |                      |            |
|      |     |      |                      |            |
|      |     |      |                      |            |
|      |     |      |                      |            |
|      |     |      |                      |            |
|      |     |      |                      |            |
|      |     |      |                      |            |
|      |     |      |                      |            |
|      |     |      |                      |            |
|      |     |      |                      |            |
|      |     |      |                      |            |

# MY PET
# DAILY CARE
# CHECKLIST

| DATE | FOOD | WATER | WALK | BATH |
|------|------|-------|------|------|
|      |      |       |      |      |
|      |      |       |      |      |
|      |      |       |      |      |
|      |      |       |      |      |
|      |      |       |      |      |
|      |      |       |      |      |
|      |      |       |      |      |
|      |      |       |      |      |
|      |      |       |      |      |
|      |      |       |      |      |
|      |      |       |      |      |

# MY PET
# IMMUNIZATION
# RECORDS

| DATE | AGE | TYPE | GIVEN BY | NEXT DUE |
|------|-----|------|----------|----------|
|      |     |      |          |          |
|      |     |      |          |          |
|      |     |      |          |          |
|      |     |      |          |          |
|      |     |      |          |          |
|      |     |      |          |          |
|      |     |      |          |          |
|      |     |      |          |          |
|      |     |      |          |          |
|      |     |      |          |          |
|      |     |      |          |          |

# MY PET WELLNESS HISTORY

| DATE | AGE | TYPE | PHYSICAL OBSERVATION | MEDICATION |
|------|-----|------|----------------------|------------|
|      |     |      |                      |            |
|      |     |      |                      |            |
|      |     |      |                      |            |
|      |     |      |                      |            |
|      |     |      |                      |            |
|      |     |      |                      |            |
|      |     |      |                      |            |
|      |     |      |                      |            |
|      |     |      |                      |            |
|      |     |      |                      |            |
|      |     |      |                      |            |

# MY PET
# DAILY CARE
# CHECKLIST

| DATE | FOOD | WATER | WALK | BATH |
|------|------|-------|------|------|
|      |      |       |      |      |
|      |      |       |      |      |
|      |      |       |      |      |
|      |      |       |      |      |
|      |      |       |      |      |
|      |      |       |      |      |
|      |      |       |      |      |
|      |      |       |      |      |
|      |      |       |      |      |
|      |      |       |      |      |
|      |      |       |      |      |

# MY PET IMMUNIZATION RECORDS

| DATE | AGE | TYPE | GIVEN BY | NEXT DUE |
|------|-----|------|----------|----------|
|  |  |  |  |  |
|  |  |  |  |  |
|  |  |  |  |  |
|  |  |  |  |  |
|  |  |  |  |  |
|  |  |  |  |  |
|  |  |  |  |  |
|  |  |  |  |  |
|  |  |  |  |  |
|  |  |  |  |  |
|  |  |  |  |  |

# MY PET WELLNESS HISTORY

| DATE | AGE | TYPE | PHYSICAL OBSERVATION | MEDICATION |
|------|-----|------|----------------------|------------|
|      |     |      |                      |            |
|      |     |      |                      |            |
|      |     |      |                      |            |
|      |     |      |                      |            |
|      |     |      |                      |            |
|      |     |      |                      |            |
|      |     |      |                      |            |
|      |     |      |                      |            |
|      |     |      |                      |            |
|      |     |      |                      |            |
|      |     |      |                      |            |

# MY PET
# DAILY CARE
# CHECKLIST

| DATE | FOOD | WATER | WALK | BATH |
|------|------|-------|------|------|
|      |      |       |      |      |
|      |      |       |      |      |
|      |      |       |      |      |
|      |      |       |      |      |
|      |      |       |      |      |
|      |      |       |      |      |
|      |      |       |      |      |
|      |      |       |      |      |
|      |      |       |      |      |
|      |      |       |      |      |
|      |      |       |      |      |

# MY PET
# IMMUNIZATION
# RECORDS

| DATE | AGE | TYPE | GIVEN BY | NEXT DUE |
|------|-----|------|----------|----------|
|      |     |      |          |          |
|      |     |      |          |          |
|      |     |      |          |          |
|      |     |      |          |          |
|      |     |      |          |          |
|      |     |      |          |          |
|      |     |      |          |          |
|      |     |      |          |          |
|      |     |      |          |          |
|      |     |      |          |          |
|      |     |      |          |          |

# MY PET WELLNESS HISTORY

| DATE | AGE | TYPE | PHYSICAL OBSERVATION | MEDICATION |
|------|-----|------|----------------------|------------|
|      |     |      |                      |            |
|      |     |      |                      |            |
|      |     |      |                      |            |
|      |     |      |                      |            |
|      |     |      |                      |            |
|      |     |      |                      |            |
|      |     |      |                      |            |
|      |     |      |                      |            |
|      |     |      |                      |            |
|      |     |      |                      |            |
|      |     |      |                      |            |

Made in the USA
Las Vegas, NV
13 May 2024

89892626R00069